THE FIRST STEPS TO SEWING

Margaret Garland

Copyright © 2018 Margaret Garland

All rights reserved.

ISBN:9781726708760

DEDICATION

This book is dedicated to all those who dream of creating fashion their way.

It's All About You!

About the author

Margaret Garland is a self-taught seamstress who has been sewing for more than 40 years. After attending Morgan State University and Baltimore City Community College, she took her education to the next level by studying at the Paris/American School of Design in Paris, France and has participated in workshops at the famed Mood Fabric Store in New York City, NY.

Margaret is professionally experienced in Fashion Design and Doll Artistry. Her work has been published in the Soft Dolls & Animal magazine and has been presented in small boutiques in Paris and Baltimore.

Even with all that, her passion has always been teaching others how to sew. She has been a teacher for the Fashion Design Department at Baltimore City Community College and FIT in North Carolina (NCSU). Margaret is the owner of Sewfabulous Sewing School. Growing into its 6th year in Pikesville, Md. Teaching students from 7 years old to adults. Her teachings have helped students prepare for Fashion Design institutions, start their own business or just giving them the tools just to create fashions. She also volunteered to teach the elderly to sew in a nearby senior care facility. Her desire to teach has leaped out of her school and found its place in schools, hospitals, and church events!

When asked why she continues to teach this skill, her answer was "To help others succeed in their dreams of design." How did you get started?

My first garment at the age of 9, was a dress (yep, big dreamer!). It turned out a bit different than the pattern. But I wore it anyway! As I continued to learn how to sew in Junior high school, my teacher wanted me to make an apron; instead, I made a purple jumpsuit! It was beautiful! I was so proud of myself. My teacher, on the other hand, was a little upset.

Sewing has continued in my life even after High school. I continued learning about clothing construction in college, then went to a community college because its curriculum was in fashion design. I had a great instructor; she's still in my life. In fact, I got to work under her when I moved back to the states. Anyway, I moved to Germany, with my husband and daughter. We lived in Darmstadt for six years. While living there, I got to return to school. I attended the

In the Beginning

Paris /American Academy in Paris! That was an awesome school. It was truly a dream come true!

In my life of sewing, I've sewn for people, designed my own line, did fashion shows, home décor, and designed dolls. Yes, dolls. First, for my daughter Jasmine, because she loved Barbie dolls. While in Germany, the doll's clothing was expensive. So, I started making the clothes. Well, I went from Barbie clothes to sculpting dolls. My favorite doll to create was topsey turvy dolls. If you haven't heard of them, it's one doll with 2-3 or more characters in it for someone who didn't play with dolls as a child. I wasn't like most sewers that began learning how to sew by making clothes for their dolls. Yet, I found that creating the doll and their clothes was so much fun! The best part was that one of my dolls (Mary Margaret) was published in the "Soft Dolls & Animals" magazine. So, as you can tell, I love to sew.

She is a member of the following organizations: American Sewing Guild, Association of Sewing and Design Professionals, The ManneqArt Educational Committee and was an instructor for Baltimore City Community College (Fashion Design and Merchandising).

In The Beginning – The First Steps To Sewing

Table of Contents

Acknowledgments

About This Book- "In The Beginning"

I. The Anatomy of Your Machine

- Understanding the parts of the Machine
- Choosing Your Sewing Machine
- The Goodie bag!
- Learning About Your Sewing Machine
- Create a Stitch Book
- The fabulous feet
- Your Sewing Tools
- The Importance of Pressing Tools

II. The Fabrics

Choosing the Correct Fabrics
- Know your fabrics
- 12 type of Fabrics commonly used
- Understanding the Grain
- Fabric terms

III. All About the Pattern

- Purchasing your first Pattern!
- Choosing your pattern
- Pattern Selection & Measurements Chart
- Understanding the Front pattern
- Understanding the Back pattern
- Pattern Adjustments

IV. Layout Preparation

- Pattern Layout/Pin/Cut
- Understanding the Tissue Paper
- Time to Choose A Layout
- Understanding the Different Types of Layouts
- Pinning The tissue to the Fabric
- Cutting your Fabrics/pattern

V. The Final Steps –

- Transferring Marking
- Choosing the Interfacing

VI. For Your Info

- Basic Sewing Terms

VII. The Art of Hand Stitching

- Basic Hand stitching
- Types of needles for hand sewing
- Using a thimble
- The basic hand- stitching

VIII. A few Extra Helpers

- Special Supplies

Credits

ACKNOWLEDGMENTS

As always, the most crucial acknowledgment goes to my Lord. For without him, I would not be able to do what I do.

Thanks to my family whom had the patience and gave me the strength and pushed me to finish this. To Jonas, my husband, for realizing my dreams. To Jasmine, my daughter, when I had problems, I could always rely on her to help me through it. Even when she keeps making me redo something! Thank you, Baby girl!

My students, for they are why I wrote this book. They are the ones that planted the idea. They would ask (constantly) "is it done yet!
My employees, they helped keep the school rolling, so I could take the time needed to work on my book.

Most importantly to my mother, she always had my back. If it wasn't for her, I'm sure I wouldn't be where I am today.
Thanks mom!
.

About This Book- "In the Beginning"

"In the Beginning" is the first part of upcoming sewing manuals of the Sewfabulous Basic Series. It was created to help the beginner sewing student learn the first steps before they begin to sew. There are many sewing books for beginners, but I felt that you weren't told those little things that keep you from making the simplest mistakes. This book is a step by step book, from buying your first pattern to the preparations before you begin to sew.
I have been sewing for many years (I tell my students 100 years). As a sewing instructor, I've seen the many mistakes students make when they begin their journey to learning how to sew. It's not a simple task. There's a lot to learn! To me, the most important part is the first phase. Beginning with purchasing the first pattern to cutting out the pattern. Then, transferring marking and using interfacing. Choosing the correct pattern, fabrics, notions and understanding the symbols is key to sewing. It's a lot but understanding these steps are so important. As you learn these techniques, you'll find sewing can be fun and exciting. Before you get too excited, you need to know that sewing takes a lot of patience! You'll make many mistakes, taking the same seams apart more than once, cut a pattern piece out incorrectly, forgetting to purchase an item needed at the time you need it, losing a pattern piece you cut out. I could go on, but I don't want to scare you away from sewing!

Just know, sewing is truly an amazing skill to learn. To create a garment from a flat surface of fabric is amazing!

Once you begin to create your own clothes, you'll feel a sense of accomplishment. Even more, because someone will say, "I like that skirt, where did you get it"? That's the moment you know you did a great job. You'll reply, "I made it." Congratulations, you're a Sewsister!
When you begin your journey, enjoy the adventures. Read as many sewing books as you can, take classes, and join clubs. Don't limit yourself to one type of project.
There's so much more to learn. From quilting to accessories. You'll be amazed at all the different ways to create.

.

Your fashion your way!

1 THE ANATOMY OF YOUR MACHINE

Understanding the parts of the machine

There are many types of sewing machines. They may look different in some ways, but they mostly have the same basic parts and threading is the same. Below are the main parts that you will find on most

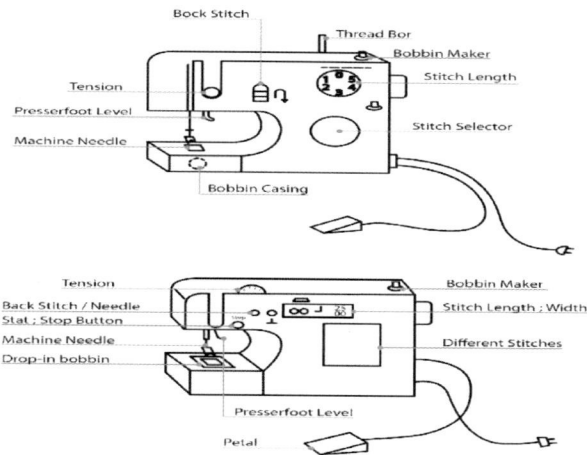

machines:

- **Tension:** this is how the pressure of the thread flows through two discs. If it's too tight' the machine stitch will have a puckering look or gathers. If too loose, the stitch will look loose. So, the higher the number, the more tension will be placed on the thread. Most machine tension will be preset. The number 4 is normally used the most.

- **Back Stitch button**: this button can vary in styles. It could be a button or a lever you push in or push down. This is used to make the machine stitch in the opposite direction. You will use your back-stitch button mainly to lock in the stitch at the beginning and the end when sewing two layers of fabric together.

Start/Stop: this is found on the newer machines. It's nice! It can be used instead of the petal, to make the machine sew. But to use it, you must disengage the petal connection. It's also good when making buttonholes, embroidered designs. It stops when the stitch is completed. It makes it easier on you and your foot!

- **Machine needle**: this is what creates each stitch. It comes in different sizes. There are machine needles for woven fabric, knit, upholstery, and silk. Remember to change it if you sew a lot. If you break your machine needle, your machine came with either a mini screwdriver or an odd shaped piece with a blunt edge (like a screwdriver). Just unscrew the extended screw, located on the inside of the shank of the needle. It will loosen so that the needle will come out. When replacing the needle, make sure you are placing it with the flat side of the needle facing away from you. Just stick it up into the hole (that you can't see!). While holder it, tighten up the screw. Tip~ place a piece of paper or fabric under the needle before removing it. So that you don't drop the needle into the base of the machine.

- **Drop-in or casing bobbin**: this is where the bobbins go. The machines with the drop-in are pretty easy to do. Remove the plastic cover, when placing the bobbin in the base (with thread on it 🪡), make sure the thread is hanging on the left side. Like the letter "P". Place into the

In the Beginning

base. Take the thread and pull to the left then right, making sure the thread falls into

- The small grove along the edge. Place the thread to the side. Now, if there a curve like canal on the left, pull thread along the canal. Some have a blade to cut the extended thread.

The next step is to get the thread to come up into the small hole below the needle. So, take the thread from the needle in your left hand and turn the flywheel (big round knob on the right side on the machine) with your right hand. Turn the wheel towards you. As the needle goes down, the thread will go around the bobbin and pick up the bobbin thread. Once it goes around the bobbin, pull the needle thread, and a loop will appear on top. Grab that loop with your right hand and pull the thread upward.

Casing bobbin- this is a round metal casing that you will place the bobbin into it. There is a slight cut on the edge of the casing. Once you place the bobbin in, pull the thread through the cut and pull it in the small rectangular open. Allow some thread to extend. Place back into the bobbin socket. Push bobbin in until you

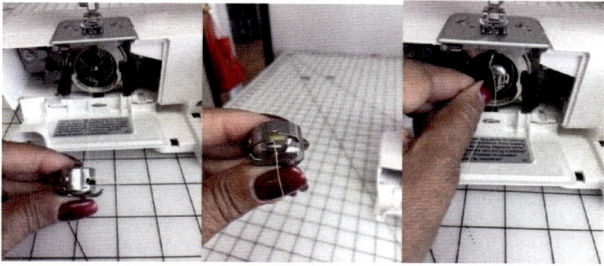

hear a click. You may have to wiggle it back and forth, till it falls into place. Like the drop-in bobbin, you will do the same left-hand - right-hand technique to bring up the bobbin thread.

- **Stitch selector**-on either the basic or digital machines will vary. Learn how to use this knob or button. You'll be able to see all the awesome stitches it can do.

- **Stitch length-** this is for the length of the stitch. It can go from nothing to really long. The normal stitch length is 2.5 when making the stitch longer; it will be considered a basting stitch.

- **Stitch width-** will vary as well. On digital machines, it's used for the zigzag stitch. But it also can change the width of other stitches too. It's also handy because it allows the needle position to change. The regular machine it is only used for the zigzag stitch.

- **Bobbin winder-** the little knob on top of the machine is where you wind up the bobbin. There is also a second part on the machine that assists the bobbin making process. It's also on the top of the machine

- But on the left side. It has a little round disc on it. Most machines thread the bobbin the same way. Take thread from spool across to the disc then around with a crisscross pattern over to the bobbin. Either put the thread into the small hole or wrap around clockwise, push bobbin to the right. Hole thread for a second. Then cut it off. The machine will stop when the bobbin is full.

- **Needle Up/Down-** This button will have machine either stop with the needle up or down. This helps sewers stay on track when topstitching, embroidery, or stitching corners. It's mainly found on digital machines.

- **Presser Foot Lever-** On some machines, in the center of the machine to the right of the needle. On others on the back of the machine, still in the needle area. It is used to lift the presser foot so that the fabric can slide under.

- **Thread Cutter-** This can be found on the left side on the machine. Or it on back of the needle shank. There are machines with automatic cutters!

Now, I just listed some of the parts of the machine. There's a lot more, depending on the type of machine you purchase. Always go over the Manual for more information about your machine.

2 Choosing Your Sewing Machine

There are so many brands to choose from. You need to know just how far you want to go, in sewing. Do you want to be a designer, seamstress, someone who wants to do alterations, a quilter or just sew for yourself?

You must do some research to decide what type of machine you want. The cost will vary, starting at $80- to thousands!

Here is a list of a few Sewing machine companies:

Brothers	Singer	Husqvarna/ Viking	Pfaff
Baby lock	Janome	Kenmore	Bernina

There is the basic sewing machine, quilting, embroidery, to name a few. If it's for a child, get the basic in case they decide sewing is not for them. If it's for an adult then purchase a machine that has more than the basics like a needle threader, 1-step buttonhole maker, speed control, blind hem foot, button foot, and a zipper foot. Then there's those bells and whistles (the other feet) that you will use to make your sewing experience even better! If the machine doesn't have all those different features or feet, you can purchase them later. Have fun choosing one!

+ The Goodie Bag!

Okay, so when you bought your machine. It came with different pressure feet and other tools. Each tool helps you sew and maintain your machine. You need to know what each item can do for you.

In the Beginning

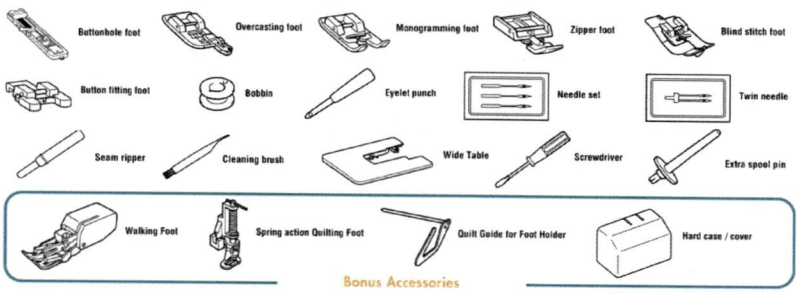

The feet are the metal or plastic objects found in the plastic pouch. If you haven't found the pouch yet, look in the base of your machine. It's right in front of the machine. It will slide off to the left (free arm base) or lift up and off, or it may be in the back of your machine. Now you may not get all the items in the picture above (or you may get more), but you should get to know the following:

Zipper foot   Buttonhole maker   Button foot   All-purpose foot

I will be going over the purpose for these feet a little later. But you may get some specialty feet too. Your sewing experience will be so much easier once you put these Feet to work for you. Remember, these feet, like the zipper foot, can have multiple uses. Even though it's mainly for attaching a zipper, it can also be used for topstitching or making/attaching piping. So, take the time to try them out!

The other tools help keep your machine running:

Machine needles   Cleaning brush

Bobbins- when purchasing more bobbins, make sure you buy the correct type. Don't be fooled by the look-alikes; your machine may not sew as well or at all.

Extra Spool pin- used to either make a bobbin without unthreading the machine. Or to hold the 2nd spool of thread, for the twin needle.

Seam ripper (your BFF)

Screwdriver- now this tool may not look like a normal screwdriver. It comes in many different shapes. Some look like a windup piece or a "T" or an oval shape. This tool makes it easier to change the machine needle or remove the screws on the plate along with the screws in the machine plate.

Notes:

_____
_____
_____
_____
_____
_____
_____
_____
_____
_____
_____
_____
_____
_____
_____

LEARNING ABOUT YOUR SEWING MACHINE

Once you've chosen your machine, you must take the time to learn all that your machine can do. There are machines for beginners, and then there are machines that will blow your minds!

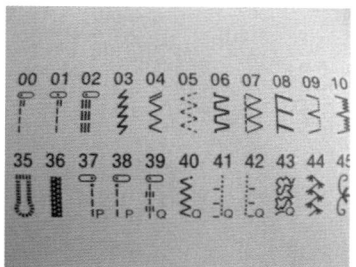

I've already explained the parts of a machine. Let's Learn about all the different stitches, feet, buttons and controls on your machine. It can be a bit overwhelming. So, take your time. I tell all my students whether your purchasing the high end or a basic machine, to do the following project to better understand the different stitches with your machine:

Create a stitch book:

- take scrap fabrics and cut 5x7 sample pieces
- Get a small notebook that will hold the sample pieces
- Create each stitch that the machine can make
- Record the settings for each stitch. If your machine is a manual (meaning, you turn knobs to change the stitch) or digital, you can make multiple styles of stitches with one design. Just by changing the stitch length or width. For example:

Zigzag stitch- can be changed from the basic style to monogram stitch just by changing the stitch length to 1 or .01. The width of the stitch can be changed just by changing the stitch width from 0(very narrow) to 5(very wide).

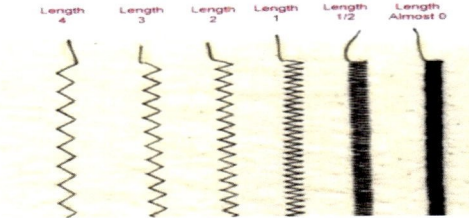

I know it sounds like a lot of work but doing this project will help you learn what your machine can do. You don't have to do it all at once but every time you use a new stitch make a sample. Also, it's exciting to see how many different designs can come from one stitch too!

In the Beginning

4. The Fabulous Feet

The following are a few of the feet that come with your sewing machine. There are at least 42 different feet that are used to make the sewing adventure easier and faster. Most machines (Brothers, Singers, and baby lock) can use these types of feet, but there are a few machines that have their own style. Meaning the shank is made differently, so the feet can only be used on their machines.

Straight Stitch Foot A straight stitch foot is used to sew simple straight stitch seams. Not only can it be used to sew regular seams, but it is also ideal for top stitching, sewing darts, and more. The small hole through which the needle passes gives support around the needle to prevent skipped stitches and puckering. This foot would be great for fine fabrics.	
Zig Zag Foot This foot is used mostly for basic sewing techniques. It can be used for all kinds of stitching, from straight stitching to decorative stitches. It can be used on all weights of fabrics which means zigzag and satin stitches.	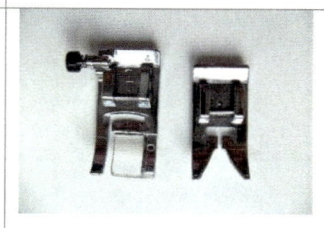

Buttonhole feet There are two types of buttonhole feet that most machines use. The shorter foot pictured is a four-step foot where the size is stitched by following the red marks. The other buttonhole foot is called a one-stepper, but there are a few steps to get a great buttonhole. With this foot, the button is placed in the back of the foot. Remember to pull down the grey arm behind the needle threader and then do the other steps!	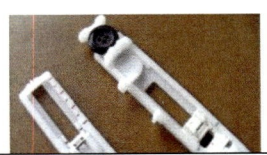 Pictured with the 4 – step button hole foot
Button Foot This foot stitches the bottom on to the garment. The button must be a 2-4-hole style. When placing the button under this foot, put feed dog down. Other machines can't lower the feed dog, so a darning plate is placed over the feed dog.	
Darning Plate Most of the newer machine would have a button on the back of the machine that makes the feed dog (the ridges teeth under the pressure foot, that makes the fabric move away from you) go down. Then there are machines that will supply you with this plate. This plate is placed over the feed dog. This is used along with the button foot and when free motion stitching is needed	
Blind hemming This foot is designed to make stitching blind hems easy and for the most part invisible when combined with the blind hem stitch. This stitch is found on most machine. To use this foot, you must practice before doing it on the main garment.	

Hemming Foot This foot is also known as a picot hem foot. A hemmed foot is used to help stitch a narrow (rolled) double hem in one pass. There are different sizes hemming feet to suit different fabric weight. To use this foot, you must practice before stitching the main garment.	

These feet are multi-purpose feet. Even though it's named to do a certain stitch, it can be used for other stitching jobs. Such as the zipper foot, it can be used to topstitch or edge stitching. So, learn the basic way first then venture off to the ways to use these feet. Whatever it takes to make your sewing adventure easier and faster, do it!

5. **Your Sewing Tools**

Using the correct tools for constructing a garment is important. Each tool will help to make sewing a lot easier. You'll find that you'll need multiples of most of the tools. I love sewing gadgets. I'm always on the lookout for new tools. Whatever makes sewing easy, is great for me.

Below is a list of most of the commonly used tools that are available to help with constructing a garment. These tools will get you started but pay attention to other tools. Once you understand how to use these tools, begin adding new tools. These are the most important sewing tools needed to start your sewing adventure.

Seam Ripper.	Bodkin
Measuring tape	Marking pencil or chalk
Straight pins	Iron & iron board
Seam gauge	Transfer wheel & carbon paper
Shears	

Each of those tools has a purpose. So, let's learn what each

can do.

Seam ripper- this tool can be your BFF in sewing. It's mainly used to remove those stitches that were sewn incorrectly. Seam rippers come in two sizes but are in many styles. There's one with a magnifier and light, a rubber grip for easy handling, and a few others. The smaller seam ripper is (for me) the best. It can get into those tight stitches that are hard to see. The larger one is good for thicker fabrics and easier to handle. Rippers are very sharp and will cut the fabric so take your time using it.

Measuring tape/rulers- A measuring tape is a long 60" tape that is used for measuring the body (bust-waist-hip to name a few) or hemming, pattern layout, drafting, and other projects. It also comes in many styles. It's not a bad idea to have more than one. Seam gauge or sewing gauge- is a ruler, usually 6 inches long. It is used to measure short spades — for example, hems. It is available in a variety of forms. The most common is an aluminum

ruler with a slider.

Straight pins- There are many types of straight pins — some designed for dressmaking, quilting or upholstery. There are

different sizes too.

Ballpoint pins- used with knits and lingerie 1- 1/16", 1- ¼", 1- 1/8" Long Pearlized pins- used for general sewing and crafts: 1-1/2"

Appliqué pins- used for position and hold appliqués 3/4"

Color ball point pins- ideal for quilt basting and home decor sewing 1-1/2"

Dressmaker pins-general purpose sewing pins. For medium weight fabric 1-1/16", 1-1/1/4"

Glass head pins- comes in ultra- Fine, Extra-Fine and regular. All are heat-resistant and multiple colors.

Pearlized pins- These pins are with a longer shaft and are for general sewing and crafts

So, you have choices but remember to read the package to make sure that package fits your sewing needs.

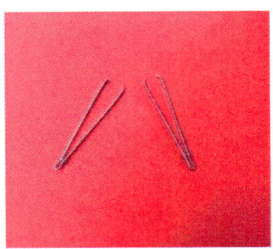

Bodkin- Is a handy tool to have. It comes in a couple of forms — the first looks like an oversized needle with a blunt point and a large eye. The other is a tweezer-like tool with a ball on one, ring in the middle and the other end a zag greed gripper. This is the one I enjoy using. The bodkin is used to pull an item such as elastic, ribbon, cording or drawstring through a casing. So much easier than the safety pin!

Shears (scissors)- Everyone knows what shears are. The important thing is to purchase a good pair. They come in many weights, styles, and abilities. Some have spring tension; different handles, and you'll find them for left and right-handers. Cutting fabric can be hard on your hands so pick wisely.

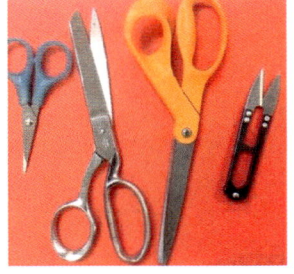

Along with the regular size scissors, you'll need a smaller pair as well. It should have a nice pointed tip. These little pointy shears help clip areas that your normal shears can't get to. It can almost work like a ripper

Transfer wheel & paper- The transfer wheel is has a multiple teeth on a wheel attached to a handle. The teeth can be serrated or smooth. It is used along with tracing paper which is carbonized paper with different color wax or chalk on one or both sides. These two tools are used to transfer markings from the pattern paper(tissue) on to the fabrics. (pleats, darts, dots, circles, triangle, etc.). When using the paper, make sure you choose the correct colors. You don't want to transfer

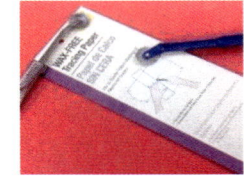

colors on to fabrics that are light color. It could show throw. Always do a sample test first before using the paper.

Marking pencil or chalk- do the same as the transfer wheel except it can come in different styles. There are soluble, disappearing, chalk, chalk-like pencils (in colors) wax. They all make marks on the fabric. Be careful with soluble and disappearing markers; they don't always do as the package say.

*FYI- Always test the colors on the fabric especially if your fabric is white. It can show through the fabric or leave a shadow behind.

Machine Needles- Sewing machines normally come with extra machine needles. But you will need to purchase more eventually. They come in different sizes and types. I'll list a few: Ballpoint- used for knits Sizes: 70/10-100/16

Universal – normally used for woven fabrics- Sizes from 11-18 (11 being the most used size)

Sharp   Denim/jeans
Twin needles   Specialty Needles
Machine Embroidery   Butterfly
Leather   Metallic

Iron & ironing board- I'm sure there's a few of you that don't iron. Sewing requires a lot of pressing. So, you need a steam iron and a nice size ironing board. There are many types of irons, so shop around. If you already have one, then no need to buy another one. Pressing your seams, hems and the overall garment is a necessity! It gives the garment a polished look. There are also pressing tools that will help to make pressing go a lot easier. The ham, roll, sleeve board, and mitt. To name a few.

The Importance of Pressing Tools

Pressing the seams are very important. It may seem like it's not that necessary, but every seam needs to be pressed open every time, to have a polish look.

When pressing, make sure you do a sample first before doing the main project. Pressing is not the same as ironing. Ironing is where you move the iron back and forth, getting all the wrinkles out of your garment. Pressing is different. The iron is moved slowly, so the stream/heat can penetrate through the fabric. This makes that seam very flat. Most of the time, you'll press on the wrong side of the fabric. This is how the garment has that polish look.

There are a few tools that help make your pressing experience easier. You already know about the iron. Remember to check the temperature before you press and have a can of spray starch close by for those hard to press area.
This following are pressing tool you can use:

 Tailor's ham- is a round like cushion that is firmly packed and has rounded corners.
It looks like a ham. It is used to press shaped areas like darts, armholes collars or seam that has a curve. It normally has a plaid wool side, and the other is cotton.

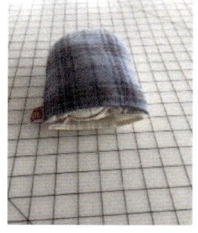 Pressing Mitt: is like the ham except it can get into hard to get areas. Plus, it can fit a sleeve board or your hand.

 Seam Roll: this tool is used just like the ham but works great for armholes, pressing seams which keep the bulk of the fabric to the sides. This keeps the iron from putting a shine on the fabric.

 Sleeve Board: this looks like two mini ironing boards attached. It is used to press small details, sleeves, Pants or necklines — anything that has curves or narrow.

 Point presser/ clapper: this made of wood. It is used for pressing corners and points. This tool is for tailoring to achieve a flat finish and Sharp points.

• Pressing Cloth: is used to prevent a shine on the
Fabric. It should be used went fusing the interfacing and keep any burn residue left on the iron from getting on the fabrics. You can purchase this cloth, but muslin is a great substitute.
Along with being inexpensive and readily available. Just purchase a ½ yard and cut it into pieces, wide enough and long enough to cover the seams. Some other fabrics you can use are:
Silk Organza - This is transparent and can take high heat.
   Cotton Twill- Natural Fabric, very good but can be bulky and opaque.
   Unbleached Muslin - I used this before I switched to the handkerchief.
Do not forget to throw the press cloth in the laundry every now and then to get rid of starch and other buildup. I also keep a small spray bottle filled with water next to my ironing table. This is useful when I am fusing interfacing. I just place the press cloth over the fabric and the interfacing and spray it generously with water. This helps the fusing process.
You could also use a man's handkerchief!

Things to remember:
- Only press fabrics with a nap like a corduroy or velvet on the reverse.
- Never press over pins, zips or buttons as this will leave a dent or mark in your fabric.
- Ensure that you keep the sole plate of your iron clean, so you don't transfer marks onto your fabric.

Notes:

CHOOSING THE FABRIC

6. **Know Your Fabrics**

When starting a sewing project, you'll begin in one of two places: either you'll have fallen in love with a pattern and need fabric to make it out of, or you'll have fallen in love with a beautiful fabric and need to find a suitable pattern to go with it.

Going to a fabric store can be so much fun! But it can also be confusing too! Choosing the correct fabric is very important. The pattern envelope will give you suggestions on what to use, but it can be very vague. So, let's try to break it down a little:

Cotton: normally used for most garments but it a large range to choose from. The definition for Cotton- is a soft white material that grows on the seeds of a tall plant and that is used to make cloth. It can be knit or woven into cloth. The two most common weaves for cotton are the plain and twill weaves. A plain weave produces fabrics like gingham, percale, chambray, and broadcloth. A twill weave is more durable and is found in denim, khaki, and gabardine.

12 TYPES OF FABRIC COMMONLY USED:

- **Cotton voile:** Voile is a lightweight, semi-sheer fabric with a great drape.
  Cotton lawn: Lawn is very similar to cotton voile but is slightly crisper.
- **Rayon Challis:** Rayon challis is a smooth, lightweight fabric. It drapes well and is slightly heavier than other lightweight fabrics, like cotton voile and cotton lawn.
- **Chambray:** Chambray is another smooth, lightweight fabric. It doesn't drape as well as rayon challis, cotton voile or cotton lawn.

- **Denim:** Denim is a heavy-weight fabric with very little drape or stretch.
- **Double gauze:** Double gauze is a unique fabric in that it is literally two layers of gauze weaved together. The double layer of fabric eradicates the main problem of sewing clothing from gauze (the sheerness) while retaining the good qualities (extremely light and breathable).
- **Knit:** In the knit fabric category, there are several types of knit, varying from lightweight to medium weight. Knit fabric is your go-to for any garment that needs to have a great deal of stretch. Patterns are designed for either woven fabric or knit fabric, and patterns sized for knit fabric will often specify the degree of stretch needed in the fabric. It will have a black bar running along the edge of the pattern then a blank bar connected to it. The knit needs to be able to stretch from the black bar to the blank bar.
- **Silk:** Silk is a lightweight, delicate fabric that drapes well. It has a slightly shimmery appearance. Silk can be slippery and more difficult to work with. It also makes a great lining fabric. This is not good for a first-time sewer!
- **Satin:** Satin can vary from lightweight to heavyweight, depending on the type of satin. Like silk, it has a glossy appearance. Also, not good for a first, time sewer!
- **Linen:** Linen is a medium-weight fabric with little elasticity (hence the wrinkles). But it conducts heat very well, which is why it's a popular choice for warm-weather anything.
- **Wool:** There are over 200 different types of wool, coming from 40 different breeds of sheep so that the weight will vary depending on the type of wool. Wool is extremely hard-wearing and versatile. It's also very warm and a good choice for colder weather garments.
- **Flannel:** Flannel is a soft, lightweight fabric. It works well for colder-temperature shirts, pants, and jackets. Know that this fabric will shrink, so it's important to wash it before sewing.

In the Beginning

This is by no means an exhaustive list, but these fabric types are a good place to start when shopping. If this is your first sewing project, then choose cotton fabrics that are easy to work with. Such as flannel, symphony or quilters cotton. Any cotton that isn't thin, shiny or shear. These fabrics can be really hard to work with.

One-way prints or plaids

One-way prints are fabrics that have a design that only goes in one direction. Just make sure your pattern pieces are running the same direction the print is going. You may have to change the layout to make it work. The last thing you want is for the print to run down one pant leg and up the other leg!

As for plaids, you must make sure the plaids are aligned. Meaning if you are making a shirt, the lines need to go across the chest from the right to the left side.

laying fabric out single layer

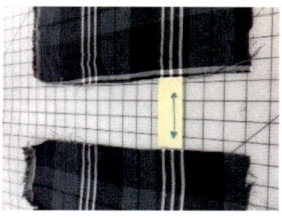

matching the plaid lines

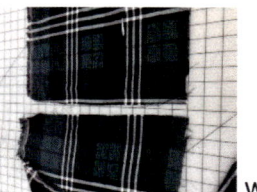

when pinning together, the lines need to be evenly balanced.

So, as you can tell when the "suggested fabric " say cotton or cotton-like fabric, it means choosing a non- stretch like fabric! Let's list a few stretches like fabrics:
There are actually 935 types of stretch fabrics!

Jersey
Fleece
Stretch velvet
Cotton jersey
Spandex

Everyone loves fabric with Lycra because of its great stretch factor. It adds comfort and ease to the figure –flattering. Like T-shirts, yoga pants, loungewear, skirts, pants, and tops

But if the pattern calls for cotton use cotton. If it calls for knit use knit. You can't do the opposite because the garment won't fit correctly (without alterations) or the construction will not look nice.

It's important to match your pattern and fabric. Think about the garments in your closet. Recall what fabric was used. Here are a few pointers:

*Pants: denim, flannel, linen, gabardine, suiting

*Shirts and blouses: cotton, cotton lawn, cotton voile, silk, chambray, flannel, gauge, challis, rayon and knit

*Skirts: linen, denim, challis, corduroy, knit

*Dresses: cotton voile, cotton lawn, satin, silk, wool, corduroy, denim, velvet

Now, no one will argue with you on your choice, but beginner sewist should follow the list until they have a better understanding of fabrics.

When purchasing your fabric, remember to buy at least ½ yards extra. Just in case the fabric shrinks, or a mistake occurs. Make sure of the width as well. Even if the salesperson says it is 45" or 60" wide, have them measure it to be sure. These days, the fabric width can be a bit short! Now, if you see a piece and love it but you can't decide what you're going to make. The rule is to buy 3 yards. This is enough to make most garments (skirt, shirt, pants). If you're tall, remember you'll need extra yardage as well. Always check the bolt on how to care for your fabric.

Shopping for fabric can be "sew" much fun!

Notes:

Understanding the Grain

When you buy fabric off the bolt (in-store or online), they unwind however many yards you want, then cut it off with scissors. Along either side (perpendicular to the cut edge) is the factory-finished edges called the selvage (or selvage). These edges are bound to keep the fabric from unraveling.

The grain of the fabric is made up of the threads running parallel to the selvage and the threads running side-to-side (perpendicular to the selvage). Here are the three types of grains.

Lengthwise Grain: Sometimes referred to as the grainline or simply grain, lengthwise grain refers to the threads that run parallel to the selvage. The technical name for these is "warp threads."

Crosswise Grain: Crosswise grain refers to the threads that run parallel to the cut edge of the fabric (the width) and so are perpendicular to the selvage. The technical name for these is "weft threads."

Bias: While technically not a grain, it's the 45° angle between lengthwise and crosswise grain. Fabric cut on the bias is stretchy, and often used anywhere you need the fabric to "bend" more smoothly around a curve, such as a collar, waistband or for covering piping, creating bias binding, or in apparel projects where you want a soft, flattering shape.

FABRIC TERMS

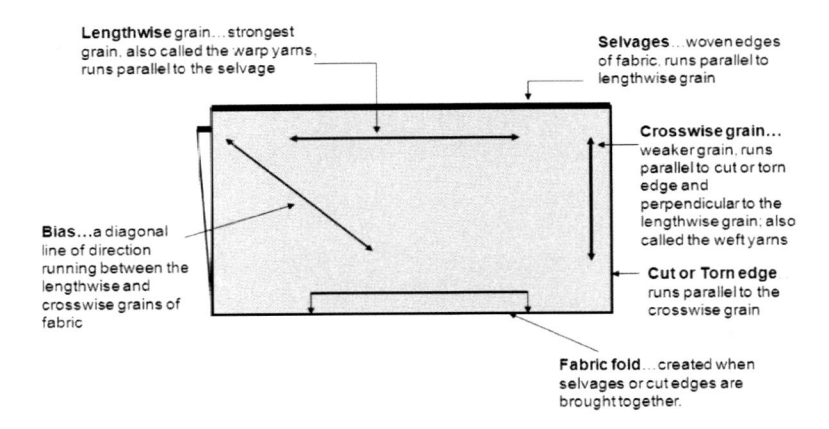

Lengthwise grain...strongest grain, also called the warp yarns, runs parallel to the selvage

Selvages...woven edges of fabric, runs parallel to lengthwise grain

Crosswise grain...weaker grain, runs parallel to cut or torn edge and perpendicular to the lengthwise grain; also called the weft yarns

Bias...a diagonal line of direction running between the lengthwise and crosswise grains of fabric

Cut or Torn edge runs parallel to the crosswise grain

Fabric fold...created when selvages or cut edges are brought together.

Remember to wash your fabric before cutting the pattern out. Check the top of the bolt. It will tell the fabric with and care instructions. As well as what it's made of.

FYI- create a fabric swatch book. Record the following:

The name of the fabric	How to care for the fabric
the amt. of yardage purchased	What it's made of
the width of the fabric	Attach a swatch of the fabric

In the Beginning

ALL ABOUT THE PATTERN

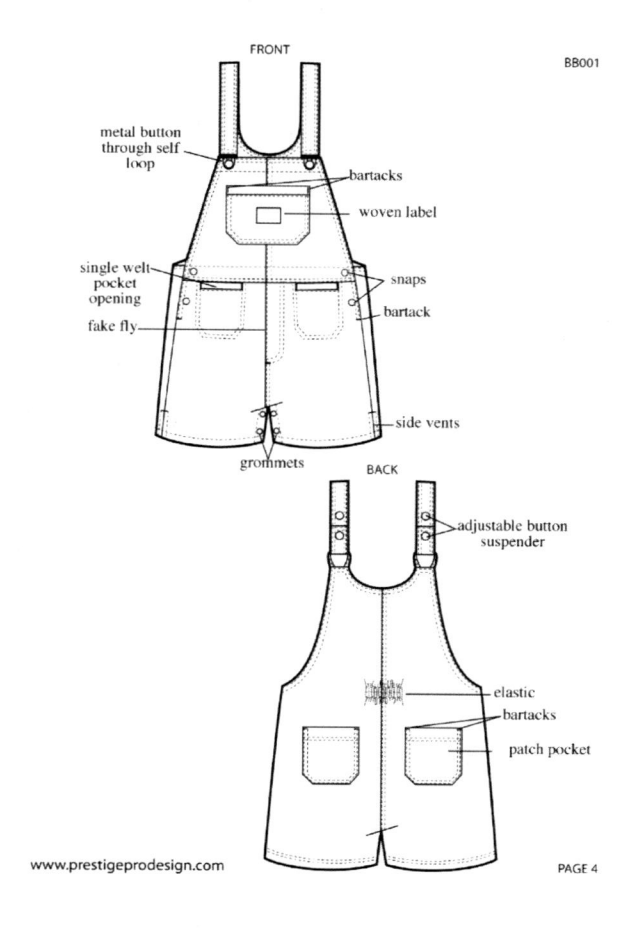

FRONT
BB001

- metal button through self loop
- bartacks
- woven label
- single welt pocket opening
- snaps
- fake fly
- bartack
- side vents
- grommets

BACK

- adjustable button suspender
- elastic
- bartacks
- patch pocket

www.prestigeprodesign.com

PAGE 4

8 **Purchasing Your First Pattern**

Purchasing a pattern for the first time can be exciting and a bit overwhelming. There are so many fabulous patterns to choose from. You want to pick the one that is simple yet fashionably you. The pattern companies will have incentives words like "Easy," "Very Easy" or "Make it in an Hour" but if you're a beginner than none of that works for you. Let's learn about the different pattern companies.

The most commonly used patterns are:

Simplicity

McCall's

Butterick

New Look

Vogue

Burda

These companies have great pattern choices, but some of them are a bit harder than others. So, when choosing a pattern, use the first three companies first then as your understanding of the technique and terminology improves, you can venture onto the others. This by no means is to say that the first three are easy. They all can be difficult. But Vogue and Burda don't give you as much instruction and pictures because they expect you to have a higher level of sewing skills to construct their patterns. Also, Burda layouts and construction is completely different from other companies. Just check out the back of their envelope!

When you choose a pattern, it's ok to pull out the layout and sewing directions to make sure you can handle it. Don't open the tissue pattern! You may not be able to return it to its original form.

9 CHOOSING YOUR PATTERN

It's so exciting to go to a fabric store to purchase all the items needed to sew your first garment. You sit and go through all the pattern books to find that perfect pattern. Here is the normal scenario: you go to the cabinet to find that pattern. You find it! You pick it up, grab that fabric you've been checking out and it's finally on sale. You check the back of the pattern for the fabric yards you need to make sure that pattern is your size. You get everything you need and go home to start a new adventure. Only you realize (after you start cutting the tissue paper) you bought the wrong size! Well, that happens to a lot of beginner sewers (OK, it still happens to upper-level sewers too!) Let's not make this mistake.

It's important to do the following when choosing a pattern:

1: After you pick a pattern, you must pay attention to the details on the front of the envelope. Make sure the construction is on your level for sewing. For example, you don't want to make a pant with welt pockets if you're a beginner. Welt pockets are for a more advanced sewer. So, look at the illustrations (if available) it lets you see those small details on how the garment is sewn.

2: **Check the size** on the front of the envelope! Just because you see it on the back doesn't mean it's in the envelope.

3: You can pull out the direction papers to see how many pieces it takes to make it and if you can understand the directions for construction.

4: Read the "**Suggested Fabrics**" for the type of fabrics to use for the garments. Now, sometimes there will be multiple garments in the envelope, and the choices can be cotton-like fabrics and knits. That means there are garments like tee shirts, tank or dress that are sewn with knit and the pants, tops that could call for cotton fabric. So, you need to read that section carefully to see what is what. Please remember, if a pattern calls for cotton, you must use cotton. If the pattern calls for knits, you must use knit. You cannot switch it! There is a good chance the garment may not sew well or fit you correctly.

5: Check the "Notions" section. These are those sewing items that you don't normally have at home (unless you've been sewing for a while). Items such as zippers, buttons, snaps, trims, bias tape, hook & eyes just to name a few — don't forget the all-purpose thread!

6: Interfacing or elastic. These items are normally found in the yardage chart. Either under the garment letter, you are making or towards the bottom of the yardage chart. (I'll talk about what interfacing is later).

Don't get fooled when the pattern says "Easy" or "Make it in 2 hours ", anything like that are sewers that have some sewing experience. I'm not saying don't try them but just take your time sewing them.

Most importantly, take your time choosing your pattern. This is the beginning of a great experience. Taking a flat fabric surface and molding it into a garment. Priceless!

A check-off list for you to take with you in is the back of this manual. So, take it with you so you won't forget anything before you get home.

Notes:

Pattern Selection & Measurement Chart

When picking your pattern, you want to make sure you are purchasing the correct size. Just because you wear a size 8 when buying your clothes, doesn't mean you wear that 8 in patterns. You probably will need a size 12. Shocking right! The pattern company has a set system, so pay attention to the measurements.

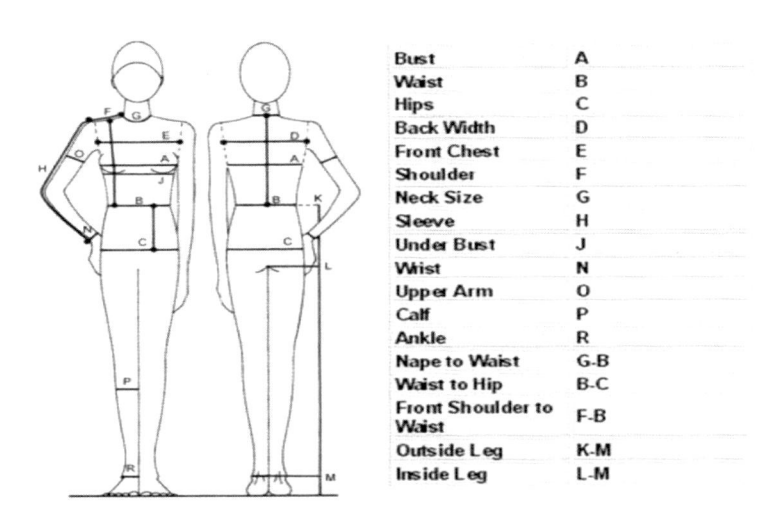

Measurement	Letter
Bust	A
Waist	B
Hips	C
Back Width	D
Front Chest	E
Shoulder	F
Neck Size	G
Sleeve	H
Under Bust	J
Wrist	N
Upper Arm	O
Calf	P
Ankle	R
Nape to Waist	G-B
Waist to Hip	B-C
Front Shoulder to Waist	F-B
Outside Leg	K-M
Inside Leg	L-M

Taking your Measurements

Measurement can be taken without assistance. But try to get help so it will go smoothly. Wear a fitted garment or a body suit. So, the measurements are correct. The chart above probably has more measurements than you really need, but these are the numbers needed to create a well-fitting garment.

Once you've picked the pattern with the correct size (found on the <u>front</u> of the envelope), check the size chart (usually found on the flap of the envelope). Use the measurements as needed for

In the Beginning

the garment your making. For example: (+ = measurements needed). Below is a size chart to assist you in figuring out your size. Record your measurements too!

Sizing Chart (inches)

SIZE	0	2	4	6	8	10	12
Bust	31"	32"	33"	34"	35"	36"	37.5"
Waist	23"	24"	25"	26"	27"	28"	29.5"
High Hip	30.5"	31.5"	32.5"	33.5"	34.5"	35.5"	37"
Hip	33.5"	34.5"	35.5"	36.5"	37.5"	38.5"	40"

SIZE	14	16	18	20	22	24
Bust	39"	40.5"	42.5"	44.5"	46.5"	48.5"
Waist	31"	32.5"	34.5"	36.5"	38.5"	40.5"
High Hip	38.5"	40"	42"	44"	46"	48"
Hip	41.5"	43"	45"	47"	49"	51"

Garment	Bust.	Waist.	Hip
Skirt		+	+
pants		+	+
Top/blouse/shirt	+	+	+
dress	+	+	+

Purchase the suggested fabric as per the yardage on the envelope. Always purchase a little more (at least a ½ yard) just in case of shrinkage, damages, or sewing mistakes. The fabrics listed will not cover every fabric, but it will, however, give you an idea of the type. Also, you cannot use knit(stretchy) fabric if the pattern calls for woven or cotton-like fabrics. The garment will not fit correctly.

Once you begin to layout your pattern on to your fabric, check the final fit symbol (found on the front pattern piece. Usually with a circle with a plus sign in the middle or just a list of sizes) to see what the final measurement numbers are. Meaning what the extra easement will be after construction. Some patterns will give an allowance number, so you'll know how it will fit. You may want to change the size you were going to cut out. An example would be if you were making a fitted "A" line skirt and your hip measurement was 28". But the final fit number was 35", the skirt might be a little looser than you wanted. You can go down a size to get the fit you want. Don't forget to check the length of pants, shirts, and sleeve especially if these are problem areas for you.

It would also be a good idea to know what body shape you are:

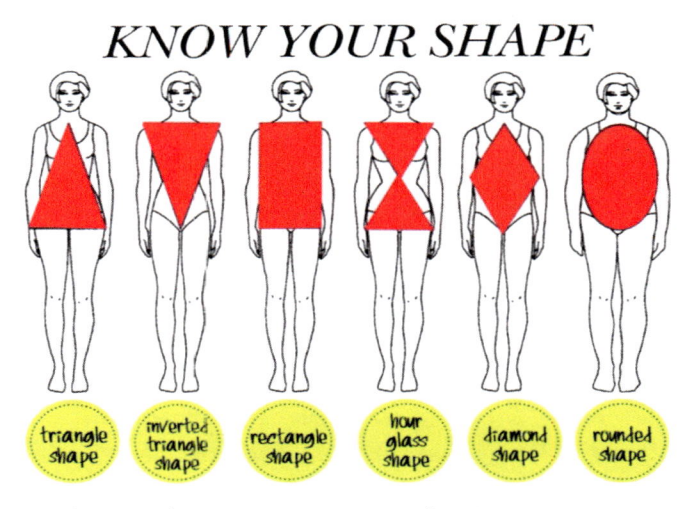

KNOW YOUR SHAPE

triangle shape | inverted triangle shape | rectangle shape | hour glass shape | diamond shape | rounded shape

So, take good measurements and enjoy creating a garment that fits you well.

Notes:

Understanding the Front of the Pattern Envelope

Picking out your pattern is easy and so much fun! There are hundreds of patterns and different companies to choose from. But it's important to pay attention to the front of the envelope. I know I've said this earlier, but I wanted you to understand the front of the pattern. You must check the do the following things before you move on to picking out the fabric.

- Check for your size
- Make sure this garment is on your level
- Pay attention to the illustrations of the garment. It will show you just what you're about to construct.
- Don't fall for the "it's so easy"- "Easy"- "Make it in 2 hours" on the pattern. It's for sewer on the Intermediate levels and above.

You can also take the information sheets out of the envelope and check out the instructions as well. At least you'll see what you're getting in to.

Understanding the Back of the Pattern Envelope

Reading the back of the pattern is important. It tells you everything you need to know so you won't purchase the wrong size, fabrics, or forget to buy the notions. Below, I have listed the items you need to pay attention to when putting it all together.

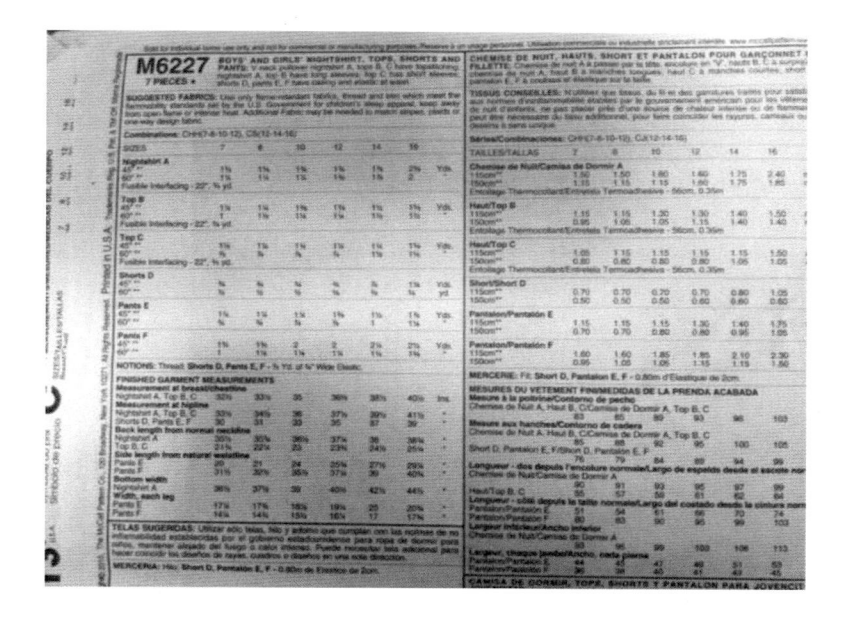

Garment description- explains exactly what technic each piece has, so you can decide if your able to construct that garment. Not all patterns will give you a description of the garments. If it doesn't, you can open the pattern and check out the instruction sheets. Just to see what you're about to get into.

Suggested fabrics- gives a list of the fabrics that will work best for that garment. It won't list every fabric, but you can use other fabrics that fall into that category. Note: if the pattern envelope has a black or blue bar going along the edge of the envelope, that means that one or all the garments are to be sewn with knit fabrics.

Fabric yardage- to know how much fabric to purchase, you'll need to know your size and fabric width (45" or 60"). Use the chart like a grid. Start from your size then go down the column to the garment letter and fabric width. You will land onto the yardage needed.

Ex. Garment D

Fabric width-45"

Size- M

Yardage needed- 2 5/8 yards (tip: always purchase about a ½ yd. more. In case your fabric shrinks, or you cut something out incorrectly). If your tall and making long pants or skirt you should purchase extra fabric as well.

Notion- these are the other items used to complete the garment, such as thread, zipper, buttons, hook & eye, etc. The thread should be an all-purpose thread. Do not use the embroidery threads (I call it the ooooo pretty thread) it's not made strong enough to hold a garment together. It normally used for embroidery designs. There is also upholstery, nylon, silk, & buttonhole threads.

In the Beginning

Size- the size is determined by your bust/ waist/ hip measurement — not the size you wear when buying clothes. Normally if you wear a size 10 for example, in ready to wear, then you'll wear a size 14/16 in patterns. Yep! It's crazy but true. So, go by the size chart when purchasing fabric. It may change with time, but we'll discuss that later.

There's one other item to check:

Interfacing- this is a stabilizer used to stiffen an area on the garment, such as pant /skirt waistband, collar or cuffs. Don't forget it!!!!!! It comes in different weights. Such as feather/ light/ medium weight. You should choose the weight that matches the weight of the fabric you've purchased. You also have the choice to purchase "sew- in" or fusible (iron-on) interfacing.

If the pattern calls for interfacing, it will be listed in the fabric yardage chart. Either below each garment listing or at the bottom of the chart with all the garments (letters) together. Like the diagram above.

So, remember the three things when getting your project:

Size - fabric type – notions

Pattern Adjustments

When selecting a pattern, getting the right size is great, but there are those of you that a have a couple of extra problems like extra-long arms or short torso or extra-long legs. Let's not forget full bust and hips. So that means "adjustments"!

Making adjustments means to take a few more measurements. The pattern won't tell you the finished arm/leg length or width. You will need to take your measurements then check it against the paper pieces. Normally the pattern paper has lengthening/shortening lines. It's usually two lines that run across the waist, crotch, hip or leg area. If you have fitting problems with your upper arm area, then you'll have to change the width from below the cap of the sleeves. You might be able to cut the larger size to give you that extra space. If you do that, then don't cut the cap in the larger size — just along the seam edge. It may give you about an inch more in width.

To length or shorten an area, measure yourself first. Follow these steps for each area:

To lengthen: Cut the tissue paper along the double lines, in the area you need to in large. Cut a strip of paper that is the added length you need to make that area, the correct length you need. You will also need to add an allowance to allow overlap. Lay the extension between the two layers and tape it together. Remeasure the length or width you needed.

To shorten:

Fold on the double lines in the area you need to shorten. Remeasure to make sure the new measurements are correct. Tape in place.

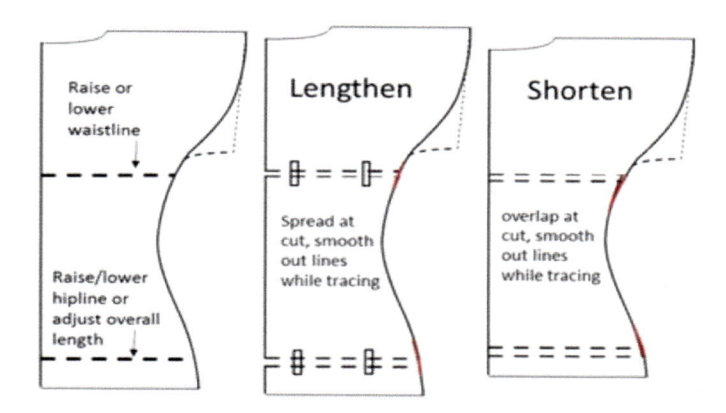

```
Raise or          Lengthen          Shorten
lower
waistline
                  Spread at         overlap at
                  cut, smooth       cut, smooth
                  out lines         out lines
Raise/lower       while tracing     while tracing
hipline or
adjust overall
length
```

For both, make sure all pieces are corrected. Of course, there are other adjustments that you may need — hips, upper arm, bustline, etc. I don't want to get in to that because you need to understand how a garment construction first. Then you can learn the other half of adjustments

LAYOUT PREPARATION

Pattern layout/Pined/Cut

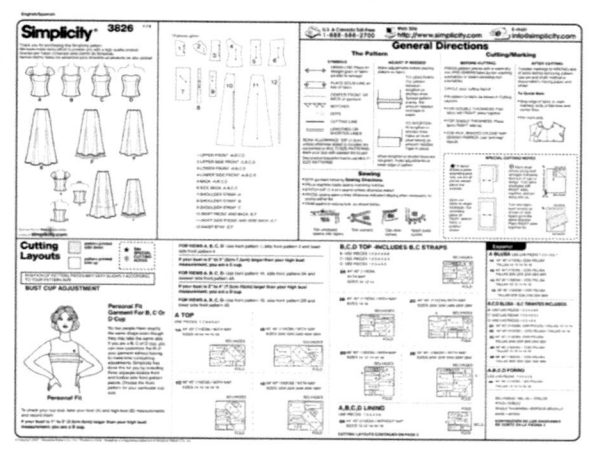

The Guide Sheet will provide you with the following information:
- Front and back view of garment
- Image of pattern pieces
- Pattern pieces required for each view
- Pattern symbols or markings

Most patterns come with multiple garments in the envelope. When you open the envelope to remove the content, you'll need the first page that will be called "pattern layout."

Most layout pages are set up in the following way: (please note that the description may vary)

The top left corner shows the garments that can be constructed

Below that should be a listing of the pattern pieces needed to construct garments

Every pattern piece has a number on it.

Below that, the numbers are listed in the order for each garment. Every tissue has a number & every number has a name.

So, you would open the tissue package, find the tissue paper will the numbers needed to construct the garment. Cut them apart but don't waste time cutting your size. You'll go too slow! You'll cut the size when you're cutting the fabric.

Understanding the Tissue paper

Once you have the pattern tissue pieces cut apart, you need to understand the information found on the tissue paper.

The usual information:

Company name

Pattern number (usually 3-4 numbers)

Name of that pattern piece (front, back, sleeve, etc.)

The number that represents the component's name.

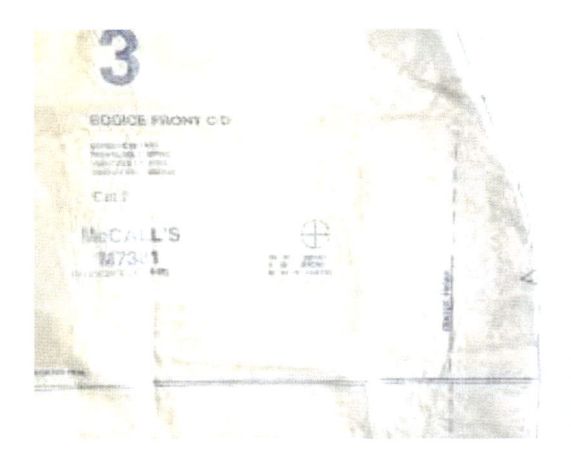

In the Beginning

How many fabric pieces needed to be cut out (1,2,4)

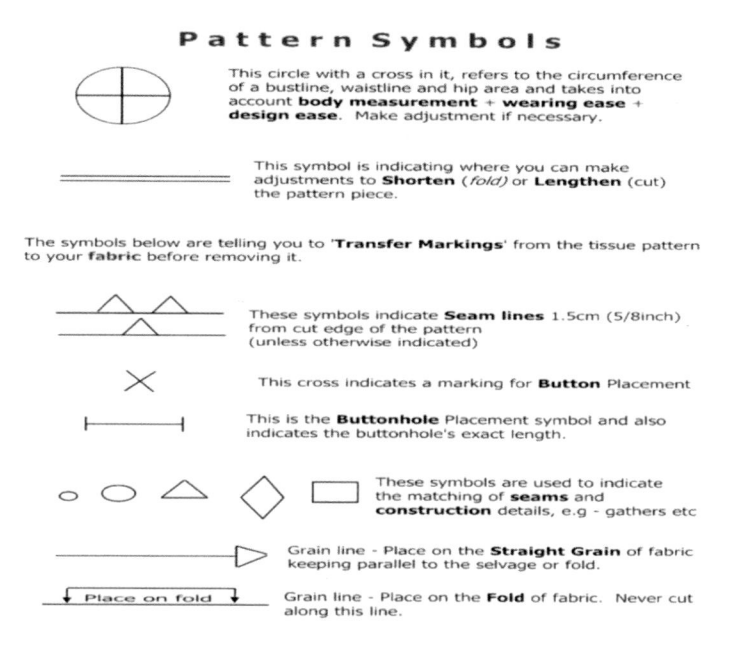

Pattern Symbols

This circle with a cross in it, refers to the circumference of a bustline, waistline and hip area and takes into account **body measurement** + **wearing ease** + **design ease**. Make adjustment if necessary.

This symbol is indicating where you can make adjustments to **Shorten** (*fold*) or **Lengthen** (cut) the pattern piece.

The symbols below are telling you to '**Transfer Markings**' from the tissue pattern to your **fabric** before removing it.

These symbols indicate **Seam lines** 1.5cm (5/8inch) from cut edge of the pattern (unless otherwise indicated).

This cross indicates a marking for **Button** Placement

This is the **Buttonhole** Placement symbol and also indicates the buttonhole's exact length.

These symbols are used to indicate the matching of **seams** and **construction** details, e.g - gathers etc

Grain line - Place on the **Straight Grain** of fabric keeping parallel to the selvage or fold.

Grain line - Place on the **Fold** of fabric. Never cut along this line.

The chart above are important symbols that the pattern could have: grainlines, cutting and transferring. It can also have some of the following symbols as well:

Darts: Lines indicating fullness and stitch lines.

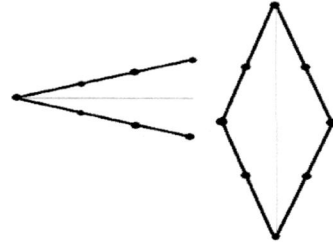

Cutting lines: multi-size patterns will have multiples lines around the pattern. Each line represents different sizes. Notice each line

is different. So, when cutting out your size, it will be easier to stay on track for your size.

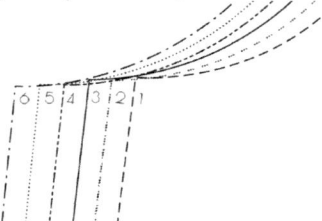

All of these symbols help you to create your garment with ease. Go over each piece, check out where if any are on the paper. The direction sheet gives you all the information, so you'll know what to do. Take the time to read the layout page. Remember most of these symbols must be transferred to on to your fabric.

Once the tissues are separated, they need to be ironed. The wrinkles need to be removed, so it lays flat on to fabric. You'll need the following tools:

Straight pins

Measuring tape

Shears

Time to choose the layout

There are three things you need to know to choose a layout.

1: Know what you're making (ex. pants A, B or C)

2: how wide the fabric is (45" or 60" wide)

3: the size you're counting out. Sometimes, you'll see abbreviations like AS- all size or no size at all.

Layouts come in different variations. Two commonly used, are the lengthwise & crosswise fold. But there are at least five different ways. First, you need to know which side the wrong and right side of the fabric is. The fabrics have two edges. One is the edge the person that cut the fabric for you and the other is the edge that runs the length of the fabric. That edge is called the selvage edge. it would have words, small holes or a fuzzy edge that doesn't fray.

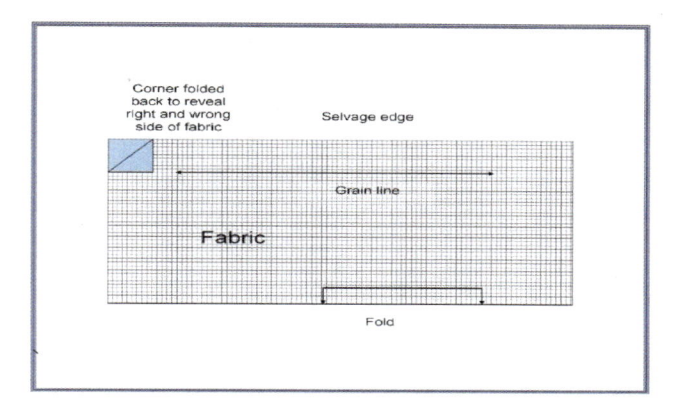

![Fabric diagram showing corner folded back to reveal right and wrong side of fabric, selvage edge, grain line, and fold]

Understanding the Different Types of layouts

The lengthwise fold(A) is where the fabric is folded in half, just like the way the fabric was bought. With the two-selvage edge is together and across from that is the fold (of course).

The Double Fold layout- (B)this is where both selvage edges are placed in the center of the fabric in the lengthwise style.

Selvage/selvage/fold- (C) still using the lengthwise style, one selvage edge is placed towards the centerfold. So, you'll have a single layer and a double layer.

Single layer-(D) the fabric would be open out flat.

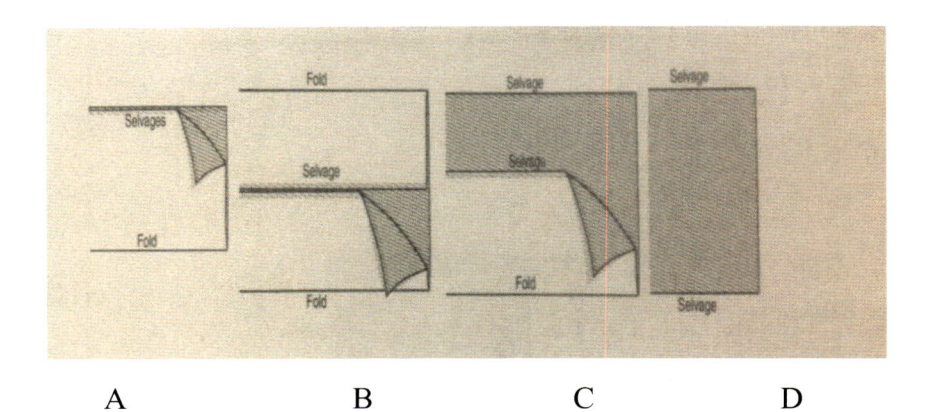

A B C D

Then there is the CrossWise fold

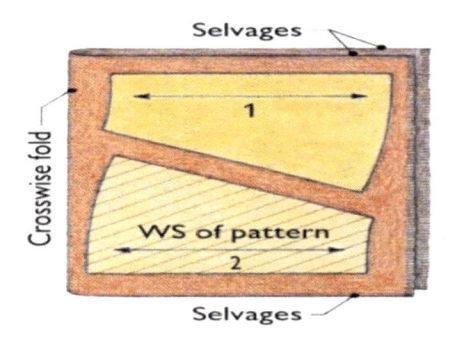

This layout is where you open the fabric out. Taking the cut two edges and bring them together. This will make the fabric much wider. If the layout picture has a * (star), then you will do a few more steps.

- Cut the folded edge making it two separate layers of fabrics.
- Place a pin into the top layer of fabric
- Lift the top layer of fabric and turn it around, so the pin is on the other end

- Keep the selvage edges going in the same direction when replacing the fabric onto the bottom layer with the wrong side up.

This is done because when folding the fabric crosswise, it causes the fibers to flow in two different directions.

For example. The lengthwise fold the fibers run in the same directions

-->-->

-->-->

but with the crosswise fold, the fibers run in two different directions.

-->-->

<--<--

So, if you have fabric with a print and it flows in the same direction, the crosswise fold will alter the flow. If you don't flip the fabric, the print will go in to different directions once you've stitched the seams. So, whether the fabric has a one, way print or solid, you must turn the top layer of fabric.

Now that we've touched on the basic layouts, it's time to place the tissue paper on to the fabric. I will go over more layouts later in the book. It's important that the pieces are placed exactly how the layout is designed. The layout is the puzzle, and the tissue paper are the pieces. You must put the puzzle together.

Pinning Pattern to Fabric

Once, you've placed a few pieces on the fabric; you must pin them into the fabric. Before you do, remember I spoke of those symbols? Well, the grainline was one of them. You'll find it on the tissue paper. The grainline is an important symbol. It needs to be measured to help keep the pattern & grain going in the same direction. Here are the steps to measure the grainline:

1: place a straight pin in one end of the grainline, place the measuring tape on that (the arrow and measure to the fold of the fabric (the fold is the straightest edge). Let's say it's 12" then measure the other end of the grainline. It must measure 12" as well.

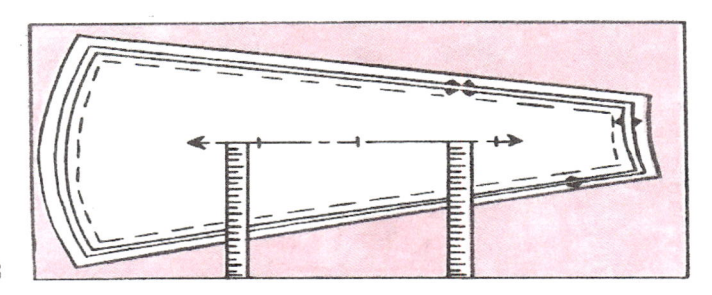

118

Once the grainline is balanced, begin pining all around that pattern. Each pin should be at least one hand width apart unless that pattern piece is small. Or curved edges. Place the pins below your size line. Not on the line, you'll have a hard time cutting with the pins in the way.

Each pattern piece must be measured then pine. Don't cut the pattern out until all pieces are pinned down.

There will be times that there may be two layouts for that garment. If so, then lay and pin wisely. You need to make sure you will have enough fabric remaining for the second layout.

There's another grainline, this symbol looks like the grainline, but the arrows are bent downward. This means the pattern must be placed on the fold of the fabric. The tissue paper will say "place on fold." After the pattern has been pinned, cut around the whole pattern except the edge on the fold.

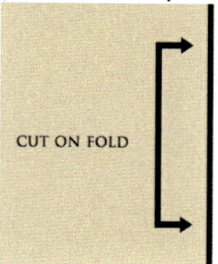

CUT ON FOLD

Please continue to read the next section before you cut the fabric!

Cutting out the pattern/ fabric

Before you start cutting the fabric and pattern, there is another symbol to pay attention to. It's called a Notch.

The Notches are truly one of the most important symbols found on the tissue paper (at least to me!). It will mostly look like a triangle. You will see it either one or two or three triangles together. The Notches have a couple uses:

1. Used as an alignment. Meaning when lining up two seams, if there's a notch on the edge, it must align with each other. That's how you'll know your stitches the correct seams together.
2. It could be the starting point where you're supposed to stitch

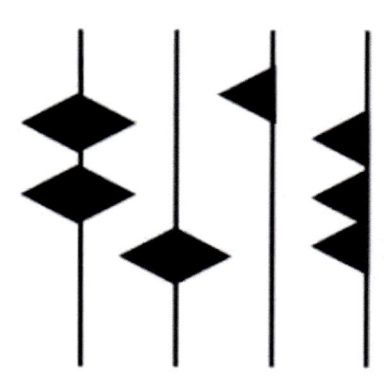

3. When cutting out the notches:
   1 notch- triangle.
   2 notches-cut it in a square shape
   3 notches cut it a rectangle shape

So, when cutting out the patterns, cut them outward, not inward. I say outward because you'll have better control with your shears. If you cut inwards, there's a chance you'll cut too deep into the pattern paper. Plus, outward will preserve the Notches on the tissue paper for the next time you use the pattern.

Cut on the size line slowly, so to stay on the lines. Remember not to cut the fold of the patterns that were pinned on the fold.

Notes:

_____
_____
_____
_____
_____
_____
_____
_____
_____
_____
_____

In the Beginning

The Final Steps!!!!!

10 TRANSFERRING THE MARKINGS

There are two more steps before constructing the garment. Transferring markings is the first.

I mentioned earlier about the marks on the tissue paper. The Dots, lines, circles, and triangles (not the same as notches). These symbols must be transferred on to the fabric. This is when you use the transfer wheel & paper. Remember, the paper comes in four colors. Choose the color that stands out, so you see it, if your fabric is a light color or sheer, you may not want to use the chalk. The color may bleed through the fabric. You don't want to see the markings on the right side of the fabric. Once you've chosen the color, fold it in half and, place the paper under the fabric and on top of the fabric, but under the tissue paper like sandwiching the fabric between the folds of the transfer paper. This is to be done on the wrong side of the fabric. Mark all the markings before you remove the tissue paper. If it's a dot, place an X in that spot: large dot- large X, small dot – small x. You must transfer darts, pleats, lines, triangles, and squares.

You can also use other marking tools, such as tailor chalk, but be careful of those disappearing inks; it may not disappear in some fabrics. Do a tester before using it.

Choosing the Interfacing

Interfacing is a textile used on the unseen or wrong side of fabrics to make an area of a garment more rigid. It can be used to stiffen or add body to the fabric. Interfacing is placed in collars, waistbands, cuffs and, buttonholes. It is placed between two layers' fabrics. Usually attached to the facings. There will be a separate layout for the interfacing pieces.

There are sew- in, fusible (woven, non- woven and knit) and different weight (feather, light, medium, and heavyweight). Choosing the correct type of interfacing is important. The pattern will tell you if your garment needs interfacing and the type needed. Usually found in the yardage area.

So how do you know what type to purchase?

Do you use sew-in or fusible interfacing and what type?

Fusible interfacing is the easiest to use. It has an adhesive on one side which can bond permanently with the fabric. It is fused by using an iron with no steam. The glue on the fusible could seep through to the right side of the fabric. Sometimes when fusing the lightweight interfacing, it could stick to the iron. Turn the iron temperature down so it won't stick. Also, pay attention when fusing the two. It could leave a little glue on the iron. Make sure to clean it off before pressing the main fabric. Fusible interfacing is suitable for most uses, but I would avoid the following fabrics:

Textured fabrics
Napped fabrics - velvet, fur
Heat sensitive – sequins, metallic, vinyl
Open weave fabrics- lace, netting

For most of these types, use the Sew-in interfacing. That means to sew it by hand! It works better.
The sew interfacing works best on fabrics that do not tolerate heat or loosely woven fabrics. Also, used for tailored garments. Sew-In interfacing is sewn on to the main fabric wrong side, its

then stitched (basted)in place by hand or by machine. Sew-In interfacing can result in a more natural shaping and drape as there is less stiffness to it. I mainly use fusible interfacing; it's easy and fast. But again, it depends on the type of fabrics. Sewing a garment can take a lot of time. So, choose wisely.

Non-woven Interfacing- is made by bonding fibers together, so there is no grainline. It can be cut it in any direction. It is suitable for most fabrics except knits

Woven interfacing- is like woven fabric, has a lengthwise grain and crosswise grain. You must make sure you're cut it the same direction as the fabric grain. So, using the non- woven is much easier.

Knit interfacing- is made by knitting the fibers together, so it has an amount of stretch to it. Knit interfacing is especially suitable for use with jerseys and other knits. If you apply woven interfacing to knit fabric, it will restrain the stretch in the knit. So, it's not a good idea!

Hair canvas- is another type of interface that is a woven type of interfacing. Used in tailoring products. Like Blazers, coats, and jackets. It is suitable for garments construction when crisp detail or firm control is wanted. Used with medium to heavy weight fabrics. It's an expensive interfacing, but if you want the polished look, it's the best interfacing to use.

Interfacing comes in different weights. There's feather, light, medium, and heavyweight. Most interfacing is from 18" to 22" wide. A lot of sewers wash their interfacing like their fabrics. Truthfully sometimes I do, and sometimes I don't. It depends on the fabric. When purchasing Heat & Bond, make sure it's for interfacing. Here are some that are for attaching appliqués.

Important tip! If it calls for it, use it! Don't try to create a garment without using interfacing.

Notes:

For Your Info

Basic Sewing Terms

The following are terms that a sewer will need to know when beginning to learn how to sew. Of course, there are a lot more but let's just start with the ones I know you'll come across first.

<u>Baste</u>- Temporary long running stitches created by hand or machine to hold the fabric in place before the final stitching.

<u>Bias-</u> true bias is a cut made on 45 degrees to the selvage. This direction allows for the stretch. BIAS refers to any line diagonal to the crosswise and lengthwise grains. Most bias patterns pieces are placed on the true bias. It's important to follow your pattern layout.

<u>Casing</u>- fabric is folded down and stitched along the turn under edge to create a tunnel to insert elastic, trim, cord or boning.

<u>Center Back</u>- (CB) represents the vertical center line of the back of a garment.

<u>Center Front</u>-(CF) represents the vertical center of the back of a garment.

<u>Clean Finish</u>- This term is used to describe to clean up the edges of a seam. (zig-zag, pink or serge are a few clean finishing.

<u>Dart</u>- Is a stitch that is created in a garment that causes that area to conform to fit that body area. It is folded and stitched along the lines to a point.

<u>Ease</u>- Has a few meanings:1-is the amount of space in a garment that allows comfortable movement. A2- a gathering stitch used to fit a longer piece of fabric to a shorter piece of fabric. 3- the difference between body measurements and garment measurements.

Edge Stitch- Straight stitching sewn very close to the edge of a seam, trim, or outer edge. Prevents edges from stretching or rolling and supports the fabric. It can also be used as a decorative stitch.

Facing- Used to finish exposed edges as a partial lining found on the center front, neckline, armhole.

Grainline- Long arrow symbol printed on the tissue pattern that is used for pattern placement. So, the pattern piece follows the lengthwise grain of the fabric.

Hem Allowance- The amount of fabric folded upward to finish the bottom of the garment. The pattern direction will say to amount to be folded, but you can fold whatever works for you. This also called the hem depth.

Hook and Eye- A two-piece fastener for clothes. Consisting of a hook that catches on to a loop or bar.

Inseam- The vertical seam inside the leg on pants.

Interfacing- Sew-In or fusible fabric used to stabilize fashion fabrics. It can also add body, reinforce, or shape a garment.

Machine baste- a stitch that is longer than the normal 2.5 length stitch. It the longest stitch that is allowed on the sewing machine. Main a temporary stitch to hold two edges together till the main stitch is done.

Notches- Found on the cutting lines of pattern tissue paper. Shaped like triangles or diamonds, indicate the points where seams should meet.

Raw Edge- The unfinished edge of the fabric.

Right Sides Together-(RST) to place the right sides of the fabrics together. Print on top of the print.

Running Stitch- An even hand stitch in which the stitches weave in and out in a dashed line.

<u>Seam Allowance</u>- The distance between the cutting and the seam line. This allowance is usually hidden inside the garment when sewn.

<u>Slip stitch</u>- Used to join two folded edges or one for folder edge to a flat surface, for an almost invisible stitch.

<u>Staystitch</u>- Machine stitches along a seamline that keeps the fabric from stretching when the seam is sewn.

<u>Topstitch</u>- A decorative stitch sewn on the right side of the garment.

<u>Waistband</u>- A band of material that encircles and fits the waistband of a garment. Such as pants and skirts.

<u>Weft</u>- The crosswise threads in a woven fabric, traveling from selvage to selvage.

<u>Without Nap</u>- this fabric the doesn't have a surface shading or texture.

<u>With Nap</u>- fabric that has a texture, pile or design that is a repeatable pattern. Fabric such as velvet or corduroy has a nap because it changes in color when smoothed in opposition directions.

<u>Wrong side</u>- Typically, the inside of a garment or the backside of the fabric.

<u>Zigzag</u>- A stitch that has width and length and looks like connected Z' s.

These are just a few sewing terms. You will come across these more often than others. Always take the time to read your glossary on the pattern instruction sheet. It will prepare you for your sewing experience

The Art of Hand Stitching
(YES, you have to hand sew!)

Basic Hand-Sewing

It's important to understand how to thread your hand needle. Hand needles come in multiple sizes. Some come long, short, large needle eye and small. When choosing your needle, make sure the needle penetrates smoothly through the fabric. You don't want to use a thick needle, for a few reasons. First, it could leave holes behind, be extremely difficult to push it through the fabric. So, don't pick the big hole because you can get the thread through it easier.

To make it easy for some of you, there are actually hand needles that have small slits to glide the thread through. A little easier but the downside is while your stitching the thread can come out.

Types of needles for hand stitching:

Sharps: these are ordinary sewing needles are available in several sizes

Darner: a long needle used for darning and basting.

Large-eye embroidery: for thicker embroidery yarns.

Small-eye embroidery: for fine embroidery yarn

Tapestry: this has a large eye canvas embroidery and is useful for threading thin elastic or ribbon

When threading the needle, there are two ways to do it. Pull the thread from the spool. Don't unroll too much. If it's too long, it can tangle up or get knots when you start sewing. This could make you start over. Use a needle threader to help put the thread through the needle hole.

You can thread the needle two ways. One would be by putting the thread through the needle hole and bring the two ends together. Tie them together with a nice size knot. This method is used to mend, hemming most types of fabrics if the fabric is thin like calico, satin or chiffon, thread with a single thin. Tie only one end. When sewing, allow only the single thread in the fabric but keep an eye on the other end, it could slip out the needles.

There is a nifty tool called a needle threader. It's a thin metal circular piece with two thin wires shaped to meet to a point. Place the wires through the hole of the needle. Put the thread through the wires and then pull the threader out the needle. Done!

Using a Thimble

Some sewers use a thimble. If your sewing heavy fabric, you may find that using a thimble may help. It can assist in pushing or pulling the needle through the fabric. To use, just place the thimble on the tip of the middle finger of the sewing hand.

There are different hand stitching techinques. Believe it or not, it's important to learn them, hand stitching can make your sewing experience easier. A lot of sewers dislike having to hand stitch. But the reality is, it can save a lot of time and frustration. Below are the basic types of hand stitching:

In the Beginning

The basic hand- stitching:

The are many types of hand-stitching's. I have only listed a few. These are the ones you'll use the most. Creating a garment can go smoothly when you do a little hand-stitching. I know a lot of you dislike hand stitching, but you'll find out that it can help make sewing easier.

Basting/Running- is a temporary stitch used to hold fabric together until the main stitch is done to hold it permanently. It is a longer stitch that is weaved the needle in and out of the fabric approximately ¼"-1/2" long. Basting is a longer stitch so its easier to remove. It can also be used a gathering stitch. The running stitch is a bit smaller in length and remains in the stitched area. It can be used

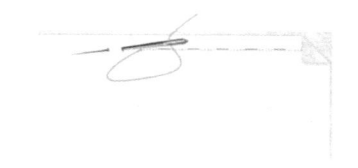

Blindstitch- is used to hem knits and bulky fabrics. Once the hem is pressed in place, turn in about a ¼" of the hem. Press. Fold back the hem a little invert the needle through the turned-in edge. Take a stitch through the main garment then into the hem edge about ¼" apart. Continue, alternating from garment to hem and keeping the stitches evening space. Remember, the stitch you take in the garment needs to be small, you're only grabbing a few threads. It's not meant the be seem on the right side.

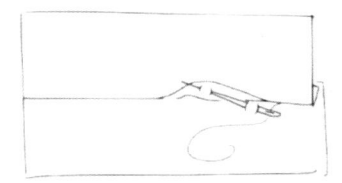

Backstitch- is a strong stitch making it perfect for securing seams and mending. Looks like a row of stitches like the machine stitch.

Each stitch overlaps the next. To do the backstitch, bring the needle through the fabric, insert it a short distance behind where it came out and bring it up through the fabric again the same distance ahead.

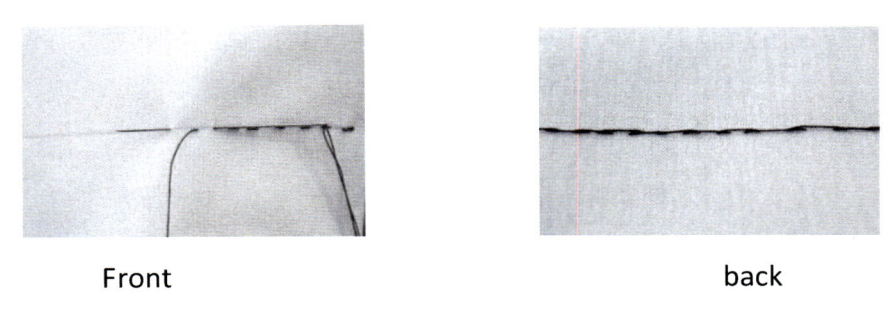

Front   back

Slipstitch- this stitch is invisible on both the inside and outside of the garment. Knot a single thread and hide the knot in the folded edge. Bring the needle, take a tiny stitch through just one or two threads in the opposite layer or fold (main fabric), then insert the needle back into the fold of the first layer. Slide the needle along inside the fold and bring it out ¼' away, continue the sequence.

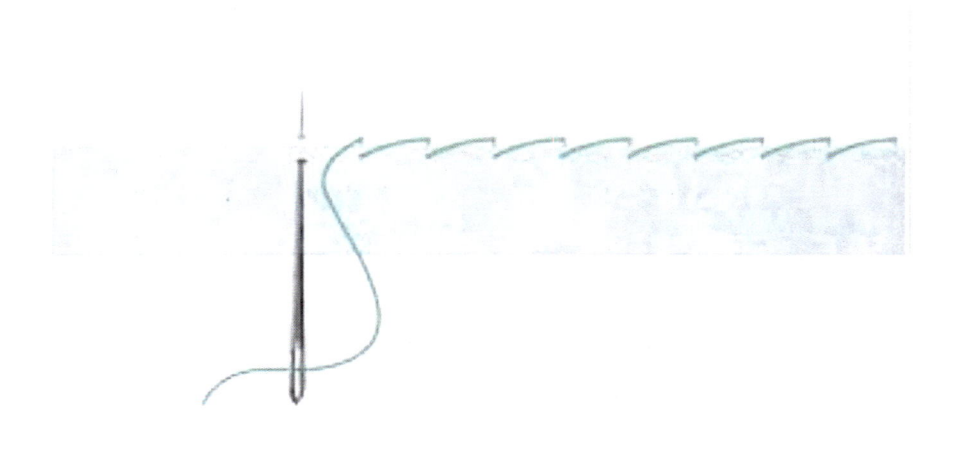

Whip Stitch: This is used to join two edges, it can also hold a raw edge neatly. To do the whip stitch, insert the needle at a right angle and close to the edge, picking up a few threads. This stitch can be used to sew seams together or hemming.

Catch stitch: is a strong hemming stitch done between the hem and the garment. Note that the stitch crosses over each other. To do the catch stitch working from left to right, take the first stitch in the fold of the hem. Fold the hem down and bring the needle up – catching a small amount of fabric then enter into the main fabric catching a small amount of fabric. Remember you don't want to take too much of the outside fabric. It's not to be seen. Just like the blind hem stitch.

This stitch can also be used as a padding stitch for tailoring and decorative.

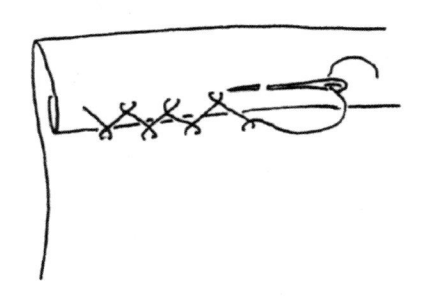

A lot of this stitch can be used for multiple sewing. There are more hand stitches to learn, but these will be a good start for beginners.

A Few Extra Helpers

Special Supplies

There are many items that help save time, which makes your sewing experience smoother. These items are an investment. When using these items, remember to add the directions and test any liquid or marking tool to make sure it works with the fabric. Here are a few of the products:

Folding Cutting board- protects the table top from scratches, stains, and pins. It also keeps the fabric from slipping off the table. Stick straight pins in it to hold an edge in place. It comes with 1" square grid that makes it easier to measure because it has measurements all around the board.

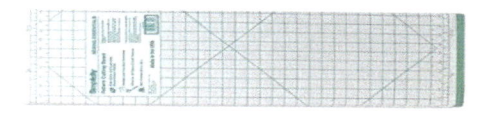

Fray Check- this is a liquid ravel protector. I'm sure there are other brands, but I like "Fray Check." A lot of fabric frays badly. If you don't serge, zigzag or do any seam finishing. It will continue to fray. And your stitch/seam will pull apart. It also helps when opening buttonholes, you may have clipped too deep into a seam causing a hole and reinforcing an area. Its dry's clear and does not wash out when launder or dry clean.

Point Turner- this tool pokes out the corners like in collars, cuffs or pockets. It can be made of wood or plastic. The point can also be used to remove basting thread and the round edge to hold sea lines open for pressing.

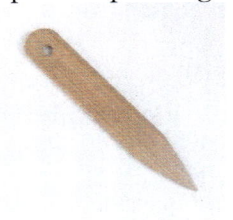

Magnetic Pin catcher- this comes in many shapes, but it's great in helping you keep your pins from falling on the floor. It can be placed by the sewing machine to catch the pins you remove from the fabric while stitching.

Weights- holds the tissue pattern in place when cutting it out. It is a great time saver. Pinning and unpinning takes up a lot of time. Weights are also helpful when pinning slippery fabrics or hard to pin fabrics. They can be purchased at your local sewing store but can pricey. I use washers from my local hardware store. There are heavy enough to hold my fabric in place. Or you can use can foods like soups.

In the Beginning

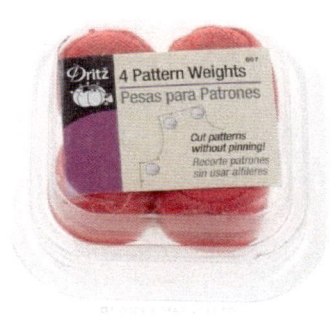

You can purchase the washers and cover or paint them! Found this on Pinterest!

Glue sticks- a great substitute for pinning or basting to hold fabric, leather, felt, trims, pockets and zippers in place before sewing. Glue sticks would wash out so don't use it if you wanted a permanent hold. There are fabrics glues that can be used for a long-term hold.

Loop turner- has a latch hook on one end to grab bias straps, tubing or cording and turn it right side out. It's better than the old way… A safety pin!

Bodkin- another tool that helps turn tube like items right side out. Really nice for inserting elastic, ribbon or cords through casings. There are two types. One has an eye to invert the elastic or trim thru, and the other is like tweezer that grips onto the item then a ring that when pushed towards the gripped end, locks the hold of the trim. This is my favorite!

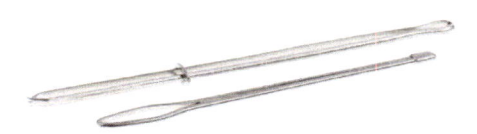

Fabric claps- looks like mini clothespins. Quilters use it to hold the edges together while seeing the ¼ seams. Now seamstress are using them as well — another great replacement for pins. Plus, if you clap them on the 1/2 edge of the fabric, you can stitch the 5/8" seam without removing the claps. Nice for those intricate areas. They come in different sizes too!

Rotary cutter- this looks like a pizza cutter. But has been used by the garment industry for years. A left or right handed person can use it. You must use it with a plastic mat called a healing board. It protects the table from being cut. Always use the special lock on it, to bring the blade down for safety.

These are some of the extras that are great to have around. There many more to have as well. So, always keep an eye open for new gadgets and gismos!

Credits

The following are websites, Blogs and or books; I used to give each sewer more information to assist them to create their garments easily. Remember to always look for more updates in construction. Build your library with these and other books, magazines, websites, Blogs, and tutorials. You'll be amazed at the amount of information that you will receive.

- Pattern layout (crosswise fold) pg.53 - Threads Magazine
- Notches pg.69 – blog.treasurie.com
- Pattern guide sheet pg. 55 – Joshua Mclaughlin
- Pattern multi size pg. 56 – tillyandthebuttons.com
    - Tissue Pattern pg.54 – Laura After Midnight- lauraaftermidnight.wordpress.com
  Pattern Layout pg. 53 – Threads: thetreadsmagazine.com
- Pattern layout (crosswise fold symbol) pg.53 – Basic pattern Symbols pg.55– yestrsdaythimble.com
- Size Chart pg.43 About – Sew Liberty – sewliberated.com
- Pattern Symbol pg. 57 – fashionsewingblog.com
- Basic Sewing Terms pgs.69-71- Allthingssewing.com
- The Art of Hand Stitching pg.73 – Sew4Home.com
        Miss sews- the basic stitches
  Sewing Clip Art- www.Kathlwenholme.com

PIN - CUT - CREATE

Achievement!

Being able to create a garment out of a flat surface of fabric is a gift. Some garments are going to give you a hard time, and the seam ripper will be your best friend. But once it's completed, you will be so proud of every accomplishment. So, keep learning, keep sewing and keep creating your style your way.

It's All About You!

Margaret Garland

In the Beginning

Made in the USA
Columbia, SC
14 August 2022